LOST PEAKLAND

LOST PEAKLAND

HISTORIC VIEWS IN AND AROUND THE PEAK DISTRICT

Doug Pickford

HALSGROVE

First published in Great Britain in 2006

British Library Cataloguing-in-Publication Data
A CIP record for this title is available from the British Library

ISBN 1 84114 551 3
ISBN 978 1 84114 551 8

HALSGROVE
Halsgrove House
Lower Moor Way
Tiverton, Devon EX16 6SS
Tel: 01884 243242
Fax: 01884 243325
email: sales@halsgrove.com
website: www.halsgrove.com

Printed and bound by CPI Bath Press, Bath.

CONTENTS

Macclesfield Field Club members pause at the gaping void of Dove Holes in Dovedale on 23 August, 1964.

INTRODUCTION

It has become a tradition within my household that, each and every Christmas, out comes a video of a BBC production of John Masefield's classic book, *A Box of Delights*. It is about a schoolboy, Kay Harker, who is given an old box by a mysterious Punch and Judy man and discovers that the box has the power to transport the bearer through space and time.

Nostalgia is lobbed at you from every angle in *A Box of Delights* – both in the original book and the video – even if you weren't around in the years between the two World Wars. It unashamedly dances in the cozy innocence which reigned in those far-off days.

What Masefield was actually writing about in his classic tale was beauty and experience. He stirs our inner being, he dredges up memories or perceptions of a world so far from our own in this consumer society: where youngsters could go safely on their own in trains, or shopping after dark, and when staple parts of the diet were gobstoppers, jam sandwiches and ginger beer. In this land that time forgot, servants were still summoned by silent bells; train sets and glove puppets were favourite toys, and the nearest thing to a Playstation was a Punch and Judy Show.

Now I, too, have been fortunate enough to have been given (or, I should say, to be assigned the responsibility for) a Box of Delights – or rather four Boxes of Delights. Equally, these have the power to transport us back through space and time, to that more innocent age. These solid oak-cased, leather-strapped boxes comprise numbered compartments which house old glass photographic plates. These three inch by three inch delicate plates provide a unique photographic record of the expanse between the township of Macclesfield in East Cheshire and across the Peak District.

They show people such as an old button maker at Flash – the highest village in England, and some claim, in Britain; a maker of musical instruments at Longnor; a one-man band tramping the Staffordshire Moorlands; a knife grinder pushing his pedal cycle across the Peakland byways, and other characters who have disappeared in those mists of time. They also show preparations for well dressings, and charabanc outings to visit ancient cockpits where labourers would once wage their hard-earned pennies on the outcome of cock fights.

They unfurl delightful scenes of hills, dales, mountains and moorlands. They reveal a world that has gone but is not forgotten, a world that will evermore remain because these priceless records on delicate squares of glass are preserved forever. They are glorious in their simplicity and beautiful in their complexity.

The slides had originally been used for lectures, both historic and geographic, and are a product of that more innocent age from the start of the twentieth century to its middle. Innocent? Certainly there were two World Wars, financial collapses and a catastrophic influenza outbreak, of that there can be no doubt but, yes, a far more innocent age. Delights were found in the simple things: nature's own, the fresh air, glorious views and our heritage. Undoubtedly it was a more innocent age, and one which many of us wish had never departed.

Would it not be glorious, therefore, if we could be transported, via a Box of Delights, to the There and Then instead of the Here and Now? Well, we can. Thanks to these amazing shots now faithfully reproduced in this book, we can take a look at the Peak District of yesteryear.

I have a number of people to thank for our being privy to this forgotten world, not least Mrs Margaret Bowen who was kind enough to think of me when she was wondering what to do with the photographic plates which had been handed down to her. Her wish was that they would be shared with as many people as possible, and when I was chatting to Roly Smith, the well-known Peak District author and former Head of Information Services at the Peak District National Park who is now Editorial Manager for Halsgrove, he suggested they should be put into book form. When I saw the high standard of publications produced by Halsgrove, I knew this would be the best way for everyone to be able to look into these Boxes of Delights.

In fact it was a Macclesfield bookseller who was responsible for recording the flora and fauna, the history, the characters and the spirit of the places in this beautiful area which they portray. The bookseller and prime mover in the collection was Margaret's father, Gerald Hine, sometimes assisted by a local solicitor, Frank Duncalf.

Gerald also amassed other, older photographs of his favourite haunts in the area which has now become the Peak District National Park and its surroundings. He also lectured on walks, illustrating these talks with these atmospheric and enigmatic glass plate photographs which he had collected over the years. When he passed on, the photographic plates, cased in those fine oak boxes, were stored away in Gerald's granddaughter's attic.

Unfortunately, not all the slides have remained, but this is no-one's fault. No doubt the ravages of time have played their part, and we must not forget that glass is, of course, a fragile medium on which to store such historic and priceless photographs. But there really was no alternative in those days; this was the best there was and this form of photography was the only medium available, so let us thank goodness the photos were taken. We would have been the poorer if they had not.

Today we can only guess at the complexity of the outings that were undertaken in order to photograph these landscapes, people and places. There can be no doubt that much hiking and tramping was involved, for the wooden camera that took these shots would not have been the miniature digital all-seeing, all-doing devices we have today. No, it was large, bulky and heavy, and demanded the use of a tripod as well. This was not a venture for the weak hearted. This was a venture for the strong, sturdy and determined. For instance, there are a few shots around Lathkill Dale. Nowadays, the walk around there can be most enjoyable and has been described as one of the finest in the Peak District, but it is a lengthy one, so no doubt the cameraman undertook the trek as a labour of love.

It appears that the sources of rivers were of particular interest, and the source of the Lathkill was readily found by the cameraman. No doubt, judging by the photos we now have, the river was followed from its source down to its meeting with the Wye at Alport. There can also be little doubt that

this proved very satisfactory, for this is definitely one of the Peak District's hidden gems and is a great walk.

The meandering River Churnet's source is also captured on camera, as is the Dane's and also the Manifold's (it is amazing how many major rivers start their journeys from our high land – the source of nature's bounty for thousands upon thousands of years). The River Wye also proved a fascination. Judging by the photographs, its course was followed from Chee Dale 3 miles east of Buxton to Miller's Dale, under Raven's Tor, in the parish of Tideswell, 4 miles north west of Bakewell.

While at Chee Dale there was obviously time for the intrepid photographer to move away from the river and climb to the surrounding crags. We know this because a splendid panoramic view of the dale is included within our Boxes of Delights. The trail goes to Monsal Dale and Monsal Head, with its superb views, and beyond. The list is seemingly endless and all 200-plus photographic plates can be seen in all their glory in this book.

Forever in our minds

Later, the intrepid duo of Gerald Hine and Frank Duncalf were among those who founded the Macclesfield Field Club, and some of the photographs here were taken during outings of that worthy society. No doubt there are many solid and sturdy memories of some of those excursions recalled in these photographs. Such memories can be addictive.

Gerald Hine (second from left), with fellow committee members of the Macclesfield Field Club. (Left to right) B. Jackson, E. E. Marsden, W. E. Evans and Miss F. M. Chapman.

For instance, I once knew an admirable gentleman by the name of Les Pace. He was a rambler long before the footpaths were opened up to those men from Manchester way, who "got all their pleasure the hard moorland way". Yes, as the famous songsmith Ewan MacColl wrote, he may have been a wage slave on Monday but he was a free man on Sunday.

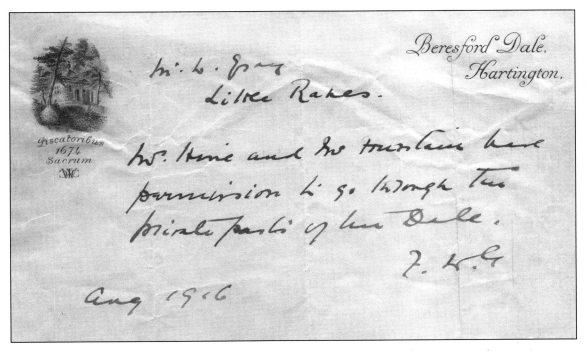

Telephone 2636   18 Castle Street
                                                        Macclesfield.

A meeting to consider the formation of a

MACCLESFIELD FIELD CLUB will be held in the

Large Sunday School, Roe Street, on

THURSDAY, 7th OCTOBER, at 8 p.m.

                                        Gerald S. Hine

A postcard sent to Miss J. Mellor of Hillside, Blakelow Road, Macclesfield, by Mr Hine in 1948 marks the formation of the Field Club.

Written permission to walk through the private sections of Beresford Dale in 1916 for Mr Hine and companion.

One particular day Les, a founder member of the Leek branch of the Ramblers' Association, and I were having a chat. He was a great talker was Les. The conversation turned to little known folklore and myths of the Peakland, a subject to which I have devoted much time, but a topic he was far more knowledgeable about than I would ever be.

During our conversation he told me how, every weekend, Bank Holiday and suchlike for the past fifty-plus years, he and his wife had discarded their workaday uniforms and donned their hiking boots, walking clothes and rucksacks. Away they would go over the Pennine moors and hills, the Derbyshire Dales, the Cheshire Plains and Staffordshire Moorlands, breathing the glorious fresh air and enjoying God's Own Country. They both loved the open air and the freedom to roam wherever they were allowed.

Mind you, the era he was talking about was that which stretched from just after the First World War, into the 1930s and then into the period when yet another World War exploded. Some walks were not available to them before the Mass Trespass and, not surprisingly, they both were proud of the fact that they took part in the defiant day that made history and opened much of the Peak District to the general public.

They carried on rambling into the 1950s and the 1960s, but gradually age began to take hold. It is as certain as the taxman, but healthy walks can ward off that evil day when walking is no longer the joy it once was. Eventually that time came for both Mr and Mrs Pace. It comes to us all but they refused to be beaten.

Even when they were both hardly able to walk at all, they would still take a journey together. How? Well, each and every evening when they went to bed they lay there, hand in hand, and one would say to the other: "Where should we walk tonight?" They would then re-live one of their favourite rambles, each talking to the other about the sights and the sounds they recalled when they were embarking on them.

One of their favourites was from Buxton to Leek, along the old Roman road that went through High Edge and Hollinsclough, sweeping over the main road close by Royal Cottage and then down between Five Clouds and Hen Cloud to Haregate and Leek. They certainly had photographic memories, did these two. They could recall most of their walks purely and simply because each and every one was special to them. They enjoyed them all. They were a delight and they relished re-living them as often as possible. So their enjoyable times remained forever in their memories. It was as simple as that.

A Field Club annual dinner. Mr Hine is standing, far left.

Looking back with happiness

A major memory which many of us who are of a certain age all share is the lurking recollection of what we were doing when President Kennedy was assassinated on 22 November, 1963. That Kennedy moment is, for me extremely easy to recall, just as Mr and Pace were able to do with their walks, for it was on that historic November evening that I met my wife, Hilary, and we have been together ever since.

It would be about the time that Mr and Mrs Pace were in the autumn of their years, but for us it was the spring. She was a young girl of sixteen, straight out of school and working behind the counter of the Cavendish Coffee Bar in Queen Victoria Street, Macclesfield, in the evenings. That coffee bar has long since gone; perhaps, like a lot of Macclesfield, it has been pulled down. One thing is for certain though, that coffee bar is now nothing more than a memory, like so many places, but it will forever remain in my recollections.

That evening of 22 November, we (and the rest of the customers of the "Cav" as the coffee bar was known by the then Bright Young Things of Macclesfield) were so engrossed in the staccato radio announcements grimly informing us that the President had been shot; then had been rushed to hospital; that a policeman had then been shot and murdered; that the President was pronounced dead (the horror unfolded bit by bit), that Hilary missed her last bus home and I, for once acting like Sir Galahad, ordered a taxi and accompanied her to her house. Oh, and I actually paid the fare as well...

As a cub reporter on the *Macclesfield Advertiser*, a local weekly newspaper in the Silk Town, I was earning very little money, the proverbial peanuts in fact, but had been told by my superiors (the Christie family, renowned as hat makers and hailing from the Hat Town of Stockport, who happened to own the Advertiser series of local weekly newspapers as a sideline) that I was being trained and should be thankful for that and for the job. In view of this fact, that particular taxi fare was at the time quite costly for me, but I have got to say that it proved a great investment in the long term!

Macclesfield was at that period, and still is for that matter, a town that sits comfortably against the East Cheshire hills. Once upon a time I had the pleasure to speak about Macclesfield – or Treacle Town as it is affectionately known – to Jean Alexander, that fine actress who is perhaps better known as *Coronation Street's* Hilda Ogden and *Last of the Summer Wine's* Aunty Wainwright. She had commenced her career in Macclesfield, as I too had done.

Miss Alexander was a part of the Adelphi Players theatre group, travelling thespians who journeyed around the Peak District in a dilapidated single-decker bus from their Macclesfield base in the early years after the Second World War. They had been formed from among a group of Conscientious Objectors during the war, who had banded together and entertained Londoners who congregated down the Underground stations during the Blitz.

Later these entertainers moved to Macclesfield where they formed the Adelphi Players, which later became the Century Theatre Company based in Manchester. Jean joined them in about 1947 or 1948 as a trainee actress and during her years with the Players toured all around the Peak District, performing at villages, hamlets and townships in halls and huts, pubs and churches in all weathers. There were times when the snow lay in 6 feet high drifts.

Once they were stranded all night close to the Cat and Fiddle Inn on the Buxton to Macclesfield road in the old banger of a bus. They were freezing cold but not only was the vehicle stuck in a snow drift, it had run out of petrol as well. Even so, she was able to look back on those days with much happiness.

She described that Cheshire town of Macclesfield to me as being rather like a snug blanket which wrapped itself around you. She was spot on. It was a cosy place to be in those days and perhaps that is why I, too, made my home in that lovely town. Some years later after I had moved on and joined the local newspaper there, the *Macclesfield Express*, I became the youngest-ever editor of a weekly newspaper in the UK.

It was a job I thoroughly enjoyed for twenty-five years of my working life. I met some astonishing people, like the editor I had the good fortune of taking over from, the late Clifford Rathbone. Clifford was known as "The Stroller" and every week he would journey around Macclesfield or further afield into the Peak District and would write about his journeys. It was his prose that brought this corner of England alive to me; he made it breathe; he made it sing; he gloried in its history and marvelled at its glory. I owe him much, not least the legacy he left me. And if anyone get can their hands on his books, do so. They will repay you handsomely in more ways than one.

Then there was another remarkable man, Cyril Dawson, who wrote a regular weekly column for the paper entitled "Nature Notes" and he called himself "Countrylover".

"Nature Notes by Countrylover" was a permanent fixture in that newspaper for nigh on thirty years. It may have been more. There was nothing Cyril did not know about the flora and fauna of the Peak District, the Cheshire Plain and the Welsh hills. He celebrated his eightieth birthday by walking to the top of Snowdon. That was the sort of chap Cyril was, and he also taught me how to enjoy the open air and in particular the area of the Peak and Plains.

Above: *The Field Club board the coach for a two-day outing to Derby, Oakham and on to Cambridge.*

Below: *In 1964 the Field Club went by coach to Thorpe then walked through Dovedale valley. A picnic lunch was then taken after passing Dove Holes before going to Hartington where tea had been arranged. Mr Hine was the leader of the outing.*

I became editor at the time that the local silk mills were in decline. Macclesfield had made its fortunes and misfortunes by virtue of the microscopic thread of the silk worm. The finished article, delicate fabric of the finest hue, had been worn by many a monarch over the centuries, but around the same time that the luckless US president received a bullet through his brain from the rifle of an assassin, man-made fibre was the order of the day and silk was in a decline.

Crimplene had been invented in Macclesfield by an Italian gentleman named Mario Nava and the silk industry flopped. His son, Christopher, often accompanied Hilary and me on walks around Buxton, Matlock and Bakewell and even today, while he looks out over the Swiss Alps from his home in Lugano, he will tell anyone who cares to ask that there is no finer scenery than that of the Peak District. Forget the Alps, they may run a close second to the Peak, but not that close.

The reason the silk trade had flourished in Macclesfield, a market town which grew up around the banks of the River Bollin – that somewhat nondescript river that flows demurely down from the hills of Wildboarclough and Wincle to the valley where Macclesfield lies – was because of the endeavours of the people who once lived and worked on those hills around the town.

It had little to do with Marco Polo and the Silk Road, the Golden Road to Samarkand and the Emperors of mighty China, but more with the wives and sisters of the hill farmers of Flash, Wildboarclough and the medieval Royal Hunting Forest known as Macclesfield Forest.

These hardy people once eked out an existence with the help of the cottage industry of button making. The men would cast the buttons from iron or from ebonised wood (the area abounded in both at one time) and the females of the homesteads would use their deft fingers to weave strands of silk round them to produce silk buttons for the gentry. This thread, it is assumed, was originally purchased from merchants who had, perhaps, trodden the Silk Road, or had purchased the thread from travellers who had used that magical and mystical route.

The Flash Buttonmakers became legendary, as did the Flash Coiners who, supposedly, made their living by counterfeiting coins by means of the instruments used to make those metal buttons. This is a long-lived legend, one that I wish was true, but has little or no substance as far as I can ascertain.

I am fortunate enough to have in my possession a great amount of research carried out by the late Frank Duncalfe – one of the gentlemen responsible for a few of the wonderful photographs in this book – and despite his best endeavours throughout most of his life, he could never discover one single resident of the area having being indicted for forgery or for passing those "flash" coins. Neither could he find any record of anyone being accused.

How I wish he was mistaken, for the stories of how these coiners would hop from county to county (Staffordshire, Cheshire and Derbyshire) at Three Shires Head to avoid the sheriff or Shire Rieve, has become the stuff of legend in many a book about the area. It is the sort of tale that should be based on fact for it is one people wish was true.

These kind of tales are a part of our national psyche: Robin Hood robbing the rich to help the poor; King Arthur's gallant knights riding out to protect a damsel in distress. Fiction becomes fact if it is repeated often enough, but I do still hope and pray that one day someone will come along with a grain of evidence to make the Flash Coiners into real life people. In fact, those myths and legends of the Flash Coiners have over the centuries transmogrified in many ways.

Some would now have it that it was illegal boxing matches that were held at Three Shires Head, and it was the bare-knuckle boys who hopped from county to county to escape the long arm of the law. Maybe it was. I would like that to be true as well. But maybe it wasn't. The historians among us would demand written proof and there is none. The romantics would demand vision and dreams, and of those there is plenty.

It has to be said that the people of Flash who I know, and have known, have in the vast majority of cases all been honest and upright citizens. I have of course come across the odd rogue but nobody's perfect and I won't go down that avenue. I say that with a purpose because my own kith and kin are products of that bleak, beautiful and divine spot – as were the ancestors of another member of the 'gang' responsible for this book, Gerald Hine.

His folk were the product of a homestead just west of Flash village which, coincidentally, is the self-same place where I and Hilary now live, named Gib Tor. That is not the only happy chance about this book, there are many instances of serendipity to be found within these pages, for truth is often stranger than fiction – especially among those daunting hills and craggy rocks around The Roches (that is the correct spelling, not with an "a" that has somehow slipped in of late), Gradbach, Upperhulme, Axe Edge and Flash.

Back in time

Gerald Hine was a bookseller and stationer in Chestergate, Macclesfield, when I started my journalistic career on the now-defunct *Macclesfield Advertiser*. That newspaper's editor was T.H. "Harry" Hayes, a doyen among local journalists, and the offices of that esteemed organ were situated directly across the road from Gerald's establishment.

I have many a recollection of Harry Hayes, who was a devout Methodist who expected his young cub reporters to behave impeccably. I also have some of Mr Hine. I regret that I never had the pleasure of meeting Mr Duncalfe.

One day my editor was walking up Mill Street – the town's main shopping street – and he spied me walking the opposite way with my girlfriend, Hilary. He said hello and I exchanged his greeting and moved on.

It was not until the following day that I was on the receiving end of his wrath, for I had been walking on the inside of the pavement that day and, as far as he was concerned, that was a disgrace. He called me into his office and, looking me straight in the eyes, said: "Douglas, I only employ gentlemen, and gentlemen never walk with a lady on the inside of the pavement. Gentlemen walk on the outside of the pavement. If I ever see you displaying such a disgraceful lack of manners again you will no longer be in my employment, young man."

He then proceeded to lecture me about how it was because horses and carriages would throw mud up from the ancient highways and a courtly gentleman would only be able to protect the lady if he was walking nearest the road.

I was suitably chastened, but a few weeks later I was asked by a somewhat older reporter if I would go to the booky's around the corner in Derby Street to pick up some winnings for him and, as misfortune would have it, Harry Hayes caught me leaving those premises complete with two £5 notes in my hands. I have never seen a gentleman's face turn from red to blue with rage before or since. It was bad enough I had even ventured into that sink of iniquity, he said, but to have profited from it was evil in the extreme. No protestation would suffice. I was destined for Hell and that was that.

It was while I was hanging on to my job at the *Macclesfield Advertiser* by the skin of my teeth that I first came to know Mr Hine. As the youngest cub reporter on that newspaper I was, more often than not, sent by my editor on most of the menial tasks and one of these was, occasionally, to buy a pencil or a rubber or something similar from the bookseller's and stationer's establishment across the way, which was owned by Mr Hine.

What an indescribably awe-inspiring and wondrous place that shop was! To my way of thinking it was straight out of Dickens. I recall there were, inside its musty-smelling interior, piles upon piles of brown paper, to be sold individually by the sheet or by the quire. Close by these sheets as an aid to wrapping a parcel (for that was, in the main, what the brown paper was used for) there stood miles upon miles of white string wrapped in balls and skeins.

Then there were the fountain pens and the scritch-scratch, wooden-handled ink pens used in my early schooldays, that were dipped in inkwells and then utilised to deliver tomes in best copperplate. There were envelopes both buff and white and writing pads embossed and lined; cardboard boxes and rows of books; elastic bands and date stamps; rubber devices to put on the end of your fingers in order to count paper money; pencils in every hardness in the entire range H to B; means of sharpening these pencils and much more. Aladdin's Cave did not contain so many treasures.

There was also, I recall, a strange smell about the place. It was a pleasurable one: a mixture of furniture wax and dust combined with ageing paper and the progression of time. I have never forgotten that heady odour but have never experienced it since. The nearest I have got to it is while visiting Calke Abbey, the home of the Harpur Crewe family near Ticknall in Derbyshire, which has been restored as a "time capsule" by the National Trust. Some of the rooms there have that similar, lingering odour.

And Mr Hine was always there behind the mahogany counter, a kindly man with a ready smile and a way of putting anyone at their ease. He appeared to me at the time to be an elderly gentleman, a product of a former generation, who wore a waistcoat with a gold Hunter watch in its pocket. Sometimes this gentleman wore a black tinted shade on his forehead, the sort I had only seen before in cowboy films. It was either bank clerks (who were being robbed by the baddies) who wore these eye shades or the Mississippi riverboat gamblers.

There are still many members of the Hine family in the wild and wonderful moorlands area around Flash, an area I like to call the Land of the Three Shires. They were – like my own family – originally squatters on the land. The law said that anyone who could build four walls and a roof and could have smoke emitting from the chimney within twenty-four hours could claim squatters' rights and could live on and farm the land.

So there we have it, a story of history and coincidence meeting, and as a result we are all able to share these amazing images of times past. Please join with me, Gerald and Frank, as we dip into our Box of Delights. I promise you will not regret it.

ONE

DELIGHTFUL CHARACTERS

We do not seem to be nurturing real 'characters' as we did in the past, and life is the poorer for it. In those far-off days, the highways and byways were walked and ridden by larger than life people such as tinkers, one man bands and the like.

And within the towns, villages and hamlets, there lived good folk who were a joy to behold because of their eccentricities, their modes of dress and the stories that grew around them. Oh that the blandness of today could be spiced with a sprinkling of these good folk.

Fortunately, thanks to our intrepid cameraman, we can still enjoy these people today. Here are just a few captured on camera forever around the Staffordshire Moorlands and the Peak District.

The Moorlands Poet, Alfred Hine of Leekfrith. Alfred's poems told of the delights of the Staffordshire Moorlands, specifically the area around the town known as "The Queen of the Moorlands" – the ancient market town of Leek – and the Meerbrook area from where he came. There are still many members of the Hine family in the Leekfrith and Meerbrook areas today, many of them farmers.

Above: This family of roving tinkers was spotted around the Wetton area, walking and cycling the highways and byways of the hills and the dales. Father, mother and son come towards the camera. On the side of the slide is written "Jack Wheelswarf". The gentleman's cycle doubles up as a knife and tool grinder. Who knows what delights the lady and lad are carrying?

One Man Band "Heather Jock", pictured at Cheddleton Heath. His hat is of tinkling bells, with drum and cymbals on his back, and he is playing an accordion. The young lad has a tambourine and was, presumably, responsible for collecting the pennies from Jock's appreciative audiences.

Opposite, bottom left: William Pickford, known as "Old Ramshaw". This larger-than-life character was a gentleman of The Roches who eventually lived at Stake Gutter Farm, now owned by the Ministry of Defence. Old Ramshaw is still remembered by a number of older residents. Because of a false accusation early in his life, he was sent to jail and on his release was forced to undertake tasks such as road mending. Often he would walk from Upperhulme to Leek and back for the markets, and at times he would sleep rough. However, he was also a fine musician and an ardent Methodist.

Opposite, bottom right: Another shot of Old Ramshaw. Note his patchwork coat and clogs.

Doctors were few and far between in the land of the Peak. Often they would be paid for their expertise with a side of ham or a few plucked chickens, a dozen eggs or so, or perhaps a piece of beef or pork. One such was Dr Haselwood, who looked after the health of people in and around Longnor.

It is believed this gentleman is a Mr Mellor, who farmed the rocky area around The Roches. He was responsible for painting The Bawdstone, a glacial erratic rock, with whitewash every year. This tradition goes back into the mists of time but each May Day, sick people were brought to the rock and crawled underneath it, to "knock the devil" off their backs. Mr Mellor is pictured by Doxey Pool, on top of The Roches ridge. Tradition has it that the water's temperature never changes, and that the pool is connected by an underground spring with the Mermaid Pool on nearby Morridge. There is also a legend of a fierce monster living within its icy waters.

Opposite top: Gerald Hine had a great affection for the Dove valley and this photograph is of Mrs Mary Horobin, who lived at Meadow Farm, Crowdicote, is one of many in his collection taken in that area. Mrs Horobin died in 1913 in her eighty-ninth year, having lived for some sixty years in a thatched homestead which later became a ruin, by the River Dove. At the time of her death she was one of the oldest tenants of the Duke of Devonshire, and had never been in a railway train in all her life. Mr Hine used to visit her when on holiday as a child in Longnor.

Opposite bottom: Mary's husband, George, feeding his sheep.

Left: Well-known Longnor resident Isaac Fiddler stands in The Square for the cameraman, around the time of the First World War. Notice the cheeky little girl in the shop door.

Below: One of the most prominent gentlemen in and around Macclesfield and the western Peak District in the time between the two World Wars was Mr R. E. Knowles, pictured with a common buzzard, with which he practised the ancient art of falconry.

The most well-known falconer in the area was the vicar of Macclesfield Forest from 1856–1889, the Rev. Gage Earl Freeman. This gentleman is pictured with one of his fine creatures – notice the hood on the bird's head.

Above: Crowds congregate in Buxton Road, Macclesfield, in 1875, to witness a feat that has now gone down in the annals of history. The landlord of the Oxford Road Tavern in the town, Captain John Alcock, had a gentleman's bet that he could walk from Buxton to Macclesfield – backwards! The crowds watch as the white-coated backwards walker starts on his trek, which he completed in something like two hours and fifteen minutes. Later, against doctor's orders, he completed the backwards walk across the moors passing the Cat & Fiddle Inn and down into the spa town some fifteen minutes faster.

Left: Captain John Alcock, the "backwards to Buxton walker".

The photographer has written "Mr Joshua Millward" at the side of this enigmatic shot. He was obviously a fine Edwardian gentleman, and it is suspected he was a resident of Longnor.

Left: "Old button maker from Flash" says the copperplate handwriting on the side of this plate. Research by Mrs Margaret Parker of Ballstone Farm, Quarnford, has revealed this bonneted lady may have been Mrs Finlow, who was pictured outside her cottage in Flash village. The button makers can be traced from the 1500s and were responsible for the silk industry being based around Macclesfield, Leek and Congleton. Their husbands or sons often made the button moulds, originally out of ebonised wood and later from metal. It is from these that the supposed counterfeit Flash coins came.

Below: Sam Sykes repairing clogs at his workshop in Longnor. This well-known chap was also the maker and repairer of musical instruments.

Here Sam Sykes is seen in the same workshop where he repaired clogs; this time he is playing a cello, one of the fine musical instruments he manufactured and also repaired.

The Peak District roads were, at one time, alive with carriers transporting goods in their horses and carts. (Today, some of the same highways are still travelled by hauliers now behind the wheel of huge lorries.) One such was William Fox, a well-known carrier between Sheffield and Buxton who later went to live in Macclesfield and is buried at Fairfield, Buxton. A portrait of the old carrier used to hang on a wall at the Setter Dog Inn, Walker Barn. Thanks to Gerald Hine's notes, we know the following about William Fox:

William Fox reckoned he had travelled about 190,000 miles. He was for six years a member of the Fairfield (near Buxton) Local Board of Guardians from which he retired, much to the regret of the ratepayers. Fox would think nothing of carrying two sacks of flour, one under each arm, from a shop to his wagon.

He went to Macclesfield from Buxton three times a week and usually drove a pair of horses. He never hurried about the delivery of goods he carried. Often he would leave Macclesfield to return to Buxton after midnight on a Saturday.

He is buried in Fairfield Churchyard and the inscription on his tombstone records that he died on 16 December, 1893, aged eighty-three years. His wife, who died in 1908, was aged eighty-seven years.

Above: The legendary Tom Steele sits outside the Hanging Gate pub at Higher Sutton near Macclesfield. Tom was landlord of the ancient inn in the 1940s and 1950s and was well-known for the hook he wore instead of a hand. It is believed he accidentally shot his hand off in a shooting accident while he was at the pub. Close inspection of this photograph shows it may have been taken before his accident, but it is hard to tell. The sign tells us the pub was a Smith's house – a Macclesfield brewery – and judging by the young girl's clothing, the photo was taken in or around the 1940s.

Right: Dr John D. Sainter wrote a book titled *Scientific Rambles Round Macclesfield* in 1878. A founder of The Macclesfield Scientific Society, this learned gentleman recorded the flora and the fauna of the Peak District and the hills around Macclesfield. He also recorded ancient sites from Arbor Low, near Youlgrave, to the Dane valley, and his book is much valued by scholars today.

Left: For countless years, Wildboarclough resident William Bullock cut and prepared rushes for the annual rushbearing service at Forest Chapel. This ancient tradition used to be carried out at most churches in the Peak District at one time, but has fallen out of favour in all but a few churches. It is still held at Forest Chapel every August, when rushes are brought to the church and the interior is decorated with them and they are also laid on the floor.

Below: The rushbearing service at St Stephen's, the chapel in Macclesfield Forest known as Forest Chapel. This was taken in the 1950s.

A portrait of James Brindley, the illiterate Derbyshire man who is known as "the Father of the Canal System." Despite his lack of education, Brindley, who was born at Tunstead near Buxton, created some of the earliest canals in the country, starting with the Duke of Bridgewater's Canal between Worsley and Manchester in 1761. He was later responsible for the Manchester–Liverpool Canal in 1766; the Grand Trunk Canal, linking Liverpool, Hull and Bristol in 1777, and the Birmingham Canal in 1768.

Two views of the Brindley Memorial on the sunken village green at Wormhill, near his home village on the White Peak plateau, near Buxton. The memorial was erected in his honour in 1895, but he was buried in the churchyard of St James at Newchapel, Staffordshire, after his death in 1772 at the age of fifty-six.

TWO

THE ANCIENT OF DAYS

From pre-history through to modern times, humankind has left its mark on the landscape and the buildings of this wonderful area.

Here we look at sights in and around the Peak District ranging from prehistoric mounds to pits used for cockfighting in the Victorian era. It is a motley collection which is both delightful and enigmatic.

A tenant of Sir Philip Brocklehurst who was farming on Barthomley Farm, Swythamley, unearthed a cache of Roman jewellery (shown here) in the late 1800s. As was his ancient right, the Lord of the Manor claimed the treasure for himself, and some of it later found its way to various museums. However, local lore has it that much of it also found its way into the pockets of the tenants, unknown to Sir Philip. Local legend also attests to the fact that where it was discovered was also the site of an ancient battle between the old English and either the Vikings or the Romans.

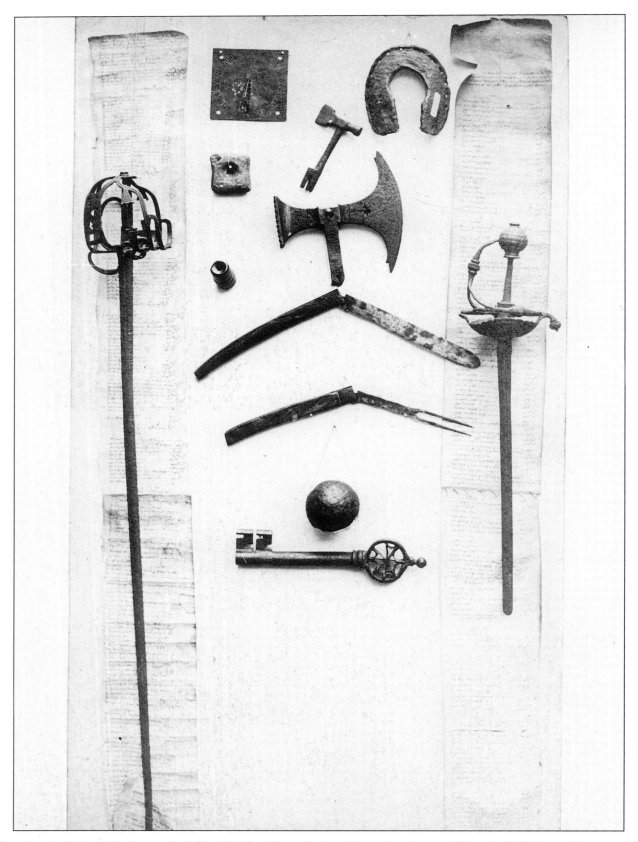

When Bonnie Prince Charlie marched from Scotland through Manchester, Stockport and Macclesfield during the 1745 rebellion, his army then followed the ancient road southwards through Sutton and Wincle, then by Bearda Hill at Swythamley and into Leek via Gun Hill. This was the old route south before the turnpike roads were built.

Legend says that Charles stopped at Swythamley Hall, the then home of the De Traffords, royal foresters originally from Trafford Park in Manchester. Some of the men also stopped at The Ship Inn at Wincle, which was on the route of the ancient byway. Either at the hall or at the inn, the Scots left behind a number of relics, some of which are pictured here. They included swords, musket shot, keys and some old newspapers telling of their escapades.

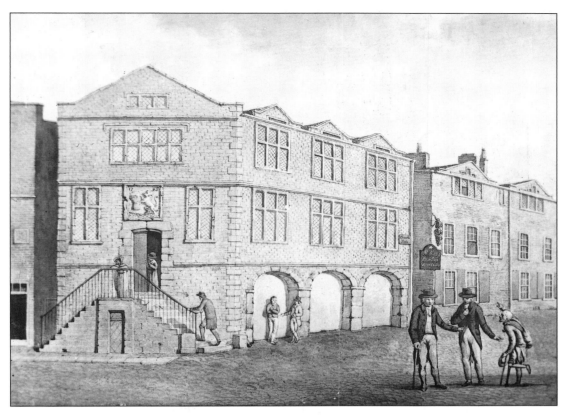

The old Town Hall, Macclesfield, as it looked in 1823.

An old toll bar cottage at Tytherington, near Macclesfield.

The toll bar house at Broken Cross, west of Macclesfield.

The ancient Sun Inn, Chestergate, Macclesfield, now demolished. The site is now occupied by a branch of the Natwest bank.

An ancient press, referred to as a coining press, was discovered in Victorian times in the well at Meg Lane Farm, Sutton. A local legend referred to the Meg Lane Coiners, who – like the notorious Flash Coiners – visited fairs and markets and distributed their counterfeit coinage. This press was supposedly used by them.

However, there is a possibility that it was the press used to make the legal coinage used by silk workers and employees of Charles Roe, who owned copper mines on Anglesey and at Alderley Edge and who had a copper works and a windmill at Macclesfield. He minted his own pennies and half pennies which could only be used at his own stores – a clever ruse.

Both sides of a carved headstone known as The Turner Stone in Eurin Lane, Rainow. This is a memorial to John Turner, a packman who perished in the snow during a winter's night in or about the year 1733. The inscription tells of the mystery of a lone footprint in the snow by the side of the body. It carries the inscription: "Here John Turner was cast away in a heavy snow storm in the night in or about the year 1733. The print of a woman's shoe was found by his side, in the snow w(h)ere he lay dead." Unfortunately, in recent times, vandals have damaged the stone.

At the top of Eurin Lane, where the Turner Stone lies, is Blue Boar Farm where another ancient stone, the Blue Boar Stone (or cross) once stood. At the time when our photographer got to it, the stone or cross was in a wall nearby. In the name "Eurin" we have, claimed the late historian Walter Smith, a short form of what might originally have been the old English "eoforwine" meaning "boar friend" or "boar protector". Today we would call such a person a gamekeeper. Markings on the stone have been highlighted in chalk.

During the 1950s, members of Macclesfield Field Club took a charabanc outing to the hills to the east of the town. Here we can see the coach, with the advert for St Bruno tobacco, as it had parked by what was termed a "cockpit" at Flash. This was a circular earthwork which was supposedly used for cock fighting. It may originally have been a bell pit, a type of early coal mine.

This cockfighting pit is a mile or so to the south at Gib Tor Lane, and is a well-documented centre of the ancient blood sport. It is said that miners and quarrymen would meet at the Royal Cottage Inn, a few yards away, and then proceed to the cockpit down Gib Tor Lane, which was well hidden from the main road and from the prying eyes of authority.

Further towards Buxton, at Knotbury, was another cockpit, again perhaps formerly a bell pit.

Even with today's modern cameras, the Neolithic stone circle and henge of Arbor Low is a difficult site to photograph in its entirety, because of its size. Here, the cameraman has almost managed to, no mean feat considering the enormity of the so-called "Stonehenge of the North". The stones of the ancient circle probably once stood upright, but today they are all lie recumbent. Field Club members are pictured inside the circle or rather, the oval, made by the limestone monoliths.

In the background is the Bronze Age barrow on the south side of Arbor Low.

The Bridestones, a 4000-year old group of ancient stones on the borders of Staffordshire and Cheshire. The megalithic monument at the pass between Wolf Lowe and a hillside called The Cloud was once a vast cairn, now all but denuded. The best comparison of how it once looked can be found at the almost intact West Kennet long barrow near to Silbury Hill and Avebury in Wiltshire.

Above: Three Mercian Saxon crosses now standing in West Park, Macclesfield. One was brought down during the late 1800s from Ridge Hall, Langley, and another from Withinshawe Lane, close to Cluelow Cross. A fourth cross or carved upright stone once stood at Wincle Grange. This was moved to Swythamley Hall for safe keeping. There are many other similar crosses in the district. One stands on top of Cluelow Cross, a man-made mound. There are also remnants of these crosses at Glossop. Perhaps Robin Hood's Picking Rods are of similar derivation.

Right: Most towns and villages had a market cross, or "mark" or "merk" stone; usually denoting the place where the "mark"et was held. Macclesfield was no exception, apart from the fact that it was removed from the Market Place and used by a farmer as a roller. Then it was taken to West Park in the town, where it stayed for many years and where it was photographed. During the 1970s, it was moved to outside the parish church in Macclesfield, a stone's throw away from its original site.

Left: There are a number of fine Saxon stone crosses at Ilam, around or in the ancient churchyard. Here is the restored rectangular cross. They are known as "crosses" because a stone shaft or collar was thought to have been fitted on them, hence a 'cross', but many think this unlikely.

Below: Another cross at Ilam, in The Ley.

Right: A round-shafted cross also at Ilam. Now very weathered, it was ornately carved in the Celtic style.

Below: A portion of a carved cross in the wall of Ilam Church.

Above: Two more fine carved crosses in the grounds of Lyme Park, near Stockport.

Left: This is believed to be the only known photograph of one of the so-called "Mercian" crosses (like the ones seen in West Park, Macclesfield) when it was still in situ at Heaton Lowe, near Rushton Spencer. It was locally known as The Ax Stone, and carries the same name as a spring – Ax Stone Spring – and was pictured some time in the 1940s on top of the ancient burial mound at Heaton Lowe. During the late 1960s, it was removed by well-known author Alan Garner, with permission, to his home near Goostrey in Cheshire.

Above: A beautiful runic cross originally from Wet Withins, a prehistoric site, but now in Eyam church-yard. It has been pointed out that the Wet Withins site, the Bull Ring at Doveholes and Arbor Low are set at the three points of a perfect triangle.

Right: Another view of the Celtic cross at Eyam.

Above: The name "Foolow" denotes a burial mound. At Foolow, a cross was erected in the 1880s, some say on the site of a previous one.

Left: The ancient bull ring at Foolow.

The motte and bailey earthworks at Pilsbury. These impressive earthworks on the hill probably from a late eleventh or early twelfth century, when a wooden castle existed here. The castle was, according to some historians, used as an administrative centre connected to the De Ferriers family (later the Earls of Lancaster), blackmiths (the farriers) who came across at the Conquest. This explains their coat of arms of three horsehoes, denoting a horse which has lost a shoe. The descendants of the De Ferriers later moved to nearby Hartington.

Above: The collection also contained this historic shot of Bunkers Hill in Macclesfield. It was situated behind the parish church and was demolished in 1907.

The old peal of bells taken from the belfry of Macclesfield Parish Church on 14 August, 1922. Pictured with the bells are J. Norbury (left) and T. Kelsall.

Opposite, bottom: Bate Hall, Chestergate, Macclesfield, which is now a public house. Local legend has it that Oliver Cromwell stayed there.

Coming as he did from Macclesfield, it is no surprise the Mr Hine's collection contained some shots of Old Macclesfield. Here we see Park Green and the elaborate fountain which went for the war effort in the 1940s.

THREE

TOURING AROUND THE ROCHES

Cistercian monks from nearby Dieulacrese Abbey named the rocky outcrop, one of the souther-most points of the Pennines, simply "the Rocks". Hardly a romantic name, but in their French Norman language it was *Les Roches*. Today, its modern spelling has become "The Roaches".

While the name may not be a romantic one, the area around and about is as beautifully formed as a Shakespearean sonnet, as full of history as the British Museum. This tract of high land stretches from Tittesworth, Meerbrook and Upperhulme in the south to Axe Edge and Flash in the north.

Nearby is the ancient market town of Longnor, another hill country abode, and a favourite place of photographer, bookseller and historian Gerald Hine. Here are some more photos from that area.

The rocky outcrops of The Roches and Ramshaw Rocks rise dramatically from the surrounding lowlands as the first western rampart of the Pennines, as seen in this photograph taken from the south. The name simply comes from the French "roches" for rocks.

The rocky outcrop of The Roches spreads across to Swythamley, where the Brocklehurst family formerly owned the land. Here we see Hanging Stone rock. Folklore has it that hangings took place here, but there is no hard evidence and in the 1800s *The Gentlemen's Magazine* wrote that the rock was the scene of sacrifices. In 1834 a forester named Hughes from the Swythamley estate was digging at its base and discovered gold and silver coins.

There are two plaques on the rock. The first is dedicated to Courtney Brocklehurst by his brother Philip, and reads in part: "Lt Col Henry Courtney Brocklehurst, 10th Royal Hussars and pilot in the Royal Flying Corps 1916–18 … killed on active service in Burma on Commano June 1942." A verse to his memory begins: "Horses he loved, and laughter, the sun, wide spaces and open air …"

Above: One of the plaques at Hanging Stone.

Right: The second plaque at Hanging Stone reads: "Beneath this rock on August 1st 1874 was buried Burke, a noble mastiff, black and tan. Faithful as a woman, braver than man. A gun and a ramble his heart's desire with a friend of his life, the Swythamley squire." This photograph shows Burke, the faithful mastiff.

Left: The mysterious chasm known as Lud's Church lies hidden in the depths of Back Forest north of The Roches above the Dane valley. There are many legends associated with this 60-foot deep landslip, the oldest of which is that it was the Green Chapel described in the classic fourteenth-century alliterative poem, *Sir Gawain and the Green Knight.* It is said to have got its name from Walter de Ludauk, a follower of Wycliff, who held services in secret there.

Below: The River Dane at Three Shires Head, where the counties of Staffordshire, Cheshire and Derbyshire converge.

Three Shires Bridge at Three Shires Head is one of the most photographed spots in the entire Peak District. In 1631 it was recorded that there were three boundary stones at this site of the meeting place of the three shires of Derbyshire, Cheshire and Staffordshire. There is no sign of them today. Historian Walter Smith wrote the following in 1923:

Of Three Shires Head strange tales are told
Of coiners, thieves and bandits bold,
Who long defied the country reeve
By hiding in some neighbouring greave;
Or, crossing o'er the border stream,
Which here with rapid waters teem,
His jurisdiction might defy
And their nefarious burdens ply.

Above, below and opposite: Three more views of Three Shires Head, where the waters of infant River Dane cascade prettily over a little waterfall below the bridge into a hollow known as Pannier's Pool, named after the many packhorse tracks which converge at this important crossroads, deep in the Staffordshire moorlands.

Gerald Hine's forefathers came from the area around The Roches known as Gib Tor. Here he has pictured one of the rocks which make up Gib Tor.

Morridge, or moorland ridge, is one of the oldest ridgeways in the British Isles. It has been used as a main route from the west to the east for thousands of years. From Morridge there is a fine view of The Roches, with the mighty pyramidical hill known as Shutlingslow on the far horizon. That hill, too, has suffered a modern-day change of spelling. The Ordnance Survey maps incorrectly name it as "Shutlingsloe".

The note on this plate says "Near Goldsitch Moss". The view looks out over The Shaws – a group of small farmsteads called Shaw Bottom, Shaw Top, Shaw Middle and Shaw House. Locally, "Shaw" is pronounced "Shay". The entire area was once the scene of open cast mining for coal. Perhaps the milk churn in the road is awaiting collection.

Again near Goldsitch Moss. Most of the farmsteads around this area were originally built under squatters' rights. Four walls, a roof and a chimney with smoke coming from it had to be built within twenty-four hours for the right of occupation to be granted. Many people would help in the construction of these buildings, moving on to the next on completion. They were small dwellings which were added to later.

Royal Cottage Inn on the Leek to Buxton road. It has been a home to the Prince family since 1960. When this picture was taken it was whitewashed but today, it is bare stone. It supposedly derives its name from Bonnie Prince Charlie staying there when the '45 Rebellion retreated from Derby back to Scotland. Nearby, at Ballstone Farm, some Scottish bonnets were discovered in the peat. They contained silk tassels, which were used to identify the different clans.

The bustling little market town of Leek is known as "The Queen of the Moorlands", and is the natural centre for the district. This photograph shows the street market in full swing in the Market Square. Leek was granted the right to hold a market by Earl Ranalf III of Chester as early as 1208, and it became a borough just six years later.

A Bedford van is parked by the New Inn at Flash – the highest village in Britain, according to locals.

Flash Church. Up to the late seventeenth century, people from around Quarnford attended Longnor Church. In 1744 a church was built at Flash by the inhabitants of Quarnford township on land given by Sir Henry Harpur. It was later rebuilt.

The highest Methodist church in the British Isles at Flash. The severe winters endured by residents of Flash is reflected in an account in the *North Staffordshire Methodist Heritage*. Mr R. O. Higginson, the Circuit Minister at Leek in the 1950s, used to ride a BSA Bantam motorbike. He was scheduled to be at Flash one winter Sunday, but when he arrived, the locals said they had not expected him because of the threat of snow. They suggested he kept a "weather eye" open through the window opposite to the pulpit, and if he saw any he should conclude and depart as quickly as possible. He did not see any snow during the service but soon after he left the snow started to fall, and the village was cut off in about twenty minutes.

A slab of gritstone acts as a "clapper" bridge over a stream at Wolf Edge, at the back of Flash Village, beyond Back o' th' Cross.

Another view of wild Wolf Edge, bordering on Knotbury. To get here, take the lane opposite Flash Church and go by the chapel; veer off on a small track on the right leading to two cottages. Follow the footpath, right, and cross the field, skirting around the western side of Oliver Hill. Rejoin the original and just before it forks turn off left and over a low hill past a small gritstone outcrop before making a steep descent down Wolf Edge to the stream below.

Goats at Hill End, Goldsitch Moss.

The Mermaid's Pool at Blakemere, with The Roches in the background. Legends tell of the mermaid who enticed travellers to their death in the bottomless pool. In fact it is only about four feet deep, and what a mermaid is doing so far away from the sea is anyone's guess. Perhaps for "mermaid" we should read "maid of the mere" or "mere maid" then all would be revealed.

Above: The area of The Roches, Morridge and beyond has been alive with packhorse men or jaggers plodding their way across the ridge roads for countless centuries. How fitting, then, that the founder of Hollinsclough Methodist Chapel in 1801 was John Lomas, packhorse man and silk trader, who successfully represented the interests of hawkers and pedlars before the House of Commons in 1785, and who later became a lay preacher.

Right The datestone on Hollinsclough Chapel, showing that John Lomas founded it in 1801.

The delightful village of Hollinsclough. Silk weaving was taking place in the village in the eighteenth century, when the silk was carried over Quarnford to Macclesfield and Leek by horse. No doubt the button-making industry was alive in the area as well.

Hollins Hill, a reef limestone ridge rising to over 1400 feet above the village of Hollinsclough to its north, is capped by a Bronze Age tumulus on its summit.

Just down the way is Longnor, the delightful former market town which, at one time, rivalled Leek as the centre for rural trading. In the nineteenth century, markets were held twice a week. It was only the coming of the railways and the development of the silk industry which made Leek a large urban development and – thankfully – left Longnor behind. Here, our cameraman captured a "flapping" – or unregulated horse race – at Longnor.

Beautiful Longnor, a photograph taken (judging by the dress) around the turn of the twentieth century.

Cycling has always been popular in the Peak District. A lone cyclist is seen in Longnor's cobbled Market Square.

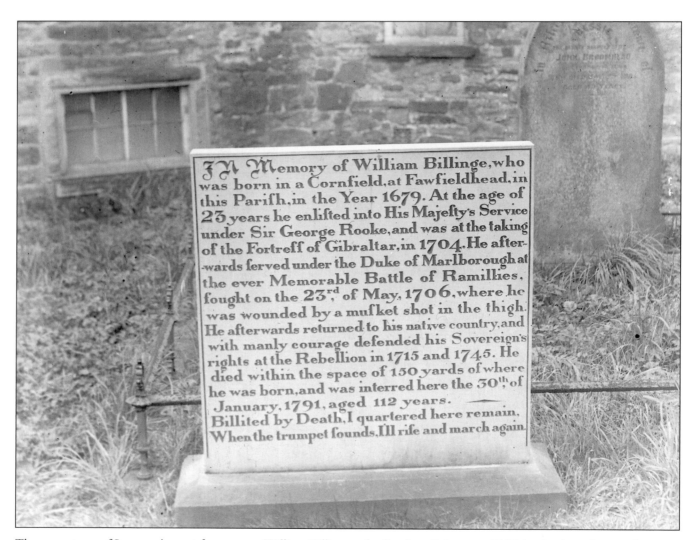

The gravestone of Longnor's most famous son, William Billinge, who lived until the age of 112, having been born at Longnor in 1679 and had a long and distinguished military career. The current gravestone is one that was copied from the fading original one in 1903.

Right: The direction stone at Longnor, pieced together again with cement.

Below: The market toll board at Longnor – a historic wooden sign showing how Longnor was once the centre of cattle and horse trading.

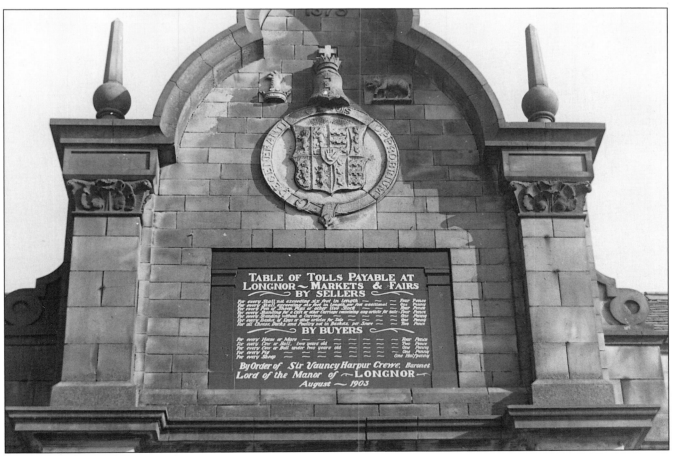

A 1940s' shot of Longnor.

The Market Hall at Longnor.

FOUR

DRESSING WELLS
AND VISITING VILLAGES

The tradition of well dressing is very much a Peak District one, although it does extend into nearby Staffordshire and Cheshire. Here we take a look at some of the activities surrounding the well dressing traditions, thanks to Gerald Hine. In 1956, Gerald went with the Macclesfield Field Club on a tour of Derbyshire's well dressings, and thanks to him we still have photographic memories of that time over half a century ago.

In Tideswell, for instance, the Wakes Week celebrations commenced when Lady Emma Cavendish, daughter of the Duke of Devonshire, crowned Tideswell's 1956 Wakes Queen, Brenda Walker. There was a sheep roast and, of course, the well was dressed. Tideswell's well dressings are traditionally ecclesiastical, and the subject that year was Wells Cathedral. Tissington and Stoney Middleton were also visited.

First stop for the Field Club and Gerald's camera in the summer of 1956 was Tissington, and this well was photographed, depicting Jesus healing the sick.

Tissington's second well was also brightly bedecked.

Tissington Hall well before its dressing.

Gerald took time out to photograph other views of Tissington. Here he captured Tissington Church.

Tissington's duck pond has attracted photographers ever since cameras were invented.

It is summer 1956, and a view of the village shows one house at least had a warming fire, judging by the smoke coming from the chimney.

Tissington Hall, home of the Fitzherberts, in 1956.

And then it was Tideswell's turn. Here, Gerald Hine captured the whole process of dressing the well from the beginning. Village men transport the main panel to the well.

Erecting the panel was delicate work.

Finally the panel, depicting Wells Cathedral, is erected.

Above: Some finishing touches are made to the centre panel.

Right: Tideswell's 1956 main panel...

Opposite: ...erected in all its glory.

The beautifully-decorated Church Avenue, Tideswell, in 1956.

Another view of Church Avenue.

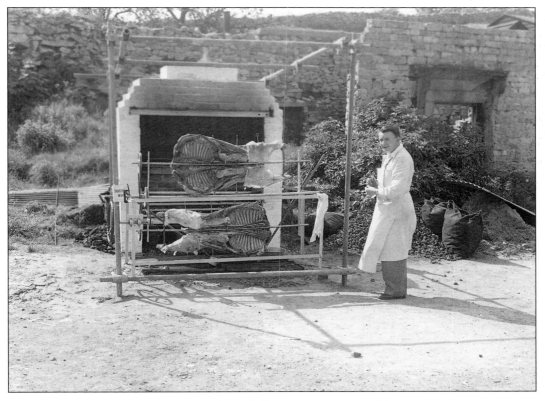

Sheep roasting at Tideswell Wakes and the well dressing ceremony, 1956.

A model of Tideswell Church, "the Cathedral of the Peak", captured on camera at the village celebrations.

The real thing: Tideswell Church in all its glory, 1956.

Four years earlier, Gerald Hine had captured the well dressing at Stoney Middleton.

"Moses in the Rushes" was the title of Stoney Middleton's other dressed well in 1952.

FIVE

THE RIVERS FLOW

The Peak District is blessed with glorious rivers flowing through glorious countryside. For centuries the beautiful rivers have attracted pilgrims and tourists alike, and one such pilgrim shortly after the Second World War was Gerald Hine, complete with camera.

Here we take a look at some of the artistic, evocative and technically-perfect photos he took, starting with the "now you see it, now you don't" disappearing River Manifold.

Stepping stones across the River Manifold, 1951.

The source of the River Manifold. This river, as with the River Dove, rises under the dark shadow of Axe Edge, that ominous hill between Quarnford and Buxton. It flows from the dark gritstone moorland, keeping its course parallel to that of the Dove, until it reaches Longnor, from where it meanders across fields into Hulme End and the area properly known as the Manifold valley.

Near to its source, the Manifold cuts a steep-sided valley in the gritstone hill.

Nields Bank, in the Upper Manifold.

The Manifold meets the River Hamps under Beeston Tor. The Hamps rises on the south side of Merryton Low, just off Morridge, and flows south through Onecote and Winkhill, then east to Waterhouses.

Except in times of very wet weather, the Manifold disappears underground as it reaches Wetton Mill and does not show itself again until it gets into Ilam Hall's parkland. Here it is shown at Rushley Bridge.

Wetton Hill, above Wetton Mill.

At Rushley Bridge.

The meandering Manifold at Rushley Bridge.

The Manifold reappears as a resurgence in the grounds of Ilam Hall.

The Leek and Manifold Light Railway was constructed in the Manifold valley in 1902 and ran from Waterhouses to Hulme End. It finally closed in 1934. Now, the trackway is a walkers' and cyclists' delight, having been tarmacked. The Manifold Track follows the river's many moods as it flows underground and overground through the valley.

Immediately south of Wetton, there is a lane which leads down into the valley of the Manifold and a small bridge and car park called Weag's Bridge. This is close to the dramatic Beeston Tor, a limestone cliff cut out by the river over the centuries. Excavations have shown that St Bertram's Cave has been occupied since the Iron Age. Higher up the valley is the dramatic and eerie Thor's Cave.

The River Manifold at Beeston Tor, photographed by Gerald Hine in August, 1951.

The Manifold at Brund Mill.

Eventually, the Manifold merges with the River Dove at Ilam. The river then becomes the Dove, the boundary between Staffordshire and Derbyshire. Here is the confluence of the two rivers.

The River Manifold at Ilam just before it joins the Dove.

Nearby are the ruins of Throwley Old Hall. This picturesque spot was chosen for a house in 1204 by Oliver de Meverell, and it remained in possession of his descendants until the 1700s. The present building was erected in 1603 by Sampson Meverell, and later passed by marriage to descendants of Thomas Cromwell, Henry VIII's confidante and minister. The ruins have recently been consolidated by the Peak District National Park. The tombs of the Meverell family can be found in Ilam Church.

It is the spring of 1956 and these lady ramblers make friends with some lambs at Castern Hall, above the River Manifold.

The head of the River Dove, on Axe Edge. The river rises close to the Leek to Buxton road and runs south for some 45 miles before joining the River Trent. For much of its course, it is the boundary between Staffordshire and Derbyshire. Walkers and ramblers are able to follow the first 20 miles with relative ease.

The source of the Dove on Axe Edge from where the river flows through Hollinsclough, Crowdicote, Pilsbury, Sheen, Hartington, Beresford Dale, Wolfscote Dale, and Lode Mill, before reaching Viator's Bridge at Milldale and entering magnificent Dovedale. Beyond Dovedale, the river joins the Manifold at Ilam, and flows on to Burton where it joins the Trent. The initials are said to be those of Izaac Walton and Charles Cotton, authors of *The Compleat Angler*.

The River Dove near its source.

The Dove at Glutton Bridge.

The Dove valley from the Sheen Road.

The Dove valley from Longnor.

The name says it all – Paradise Walk, Ilam, taken on 3 March, 1957.

The magnificence that is Dovedale, one of the most popular and visited spots in the Peak District.

A picture postcard showing some of the main attractions in Dovedale, including Ilam Rock on the left.

A delightful scene as the river flows through Dovedale.

Another shot taken by Gerald of Dovedale.

The limestone crags and meandering Dove in Dovedale.

Sheep safely graze by the River Dove in Dovedale.

Above: Washgate packhorse bridge, an ancient crossing point of the River Dove near Hollinsclough, which has a cobbled pack-horse track leading down to it.

Below: A close-up of the cobbled track crossing Washgate Bridge.

It would be nice to have the names of these Edwardian ladies pictured on a rickety wooden footbridge in Dovedale. Unfortunately we don't, but their memory can remain forever in this delightful shot. What an adventure they were having!

The River Dane – either named from the old English for tumbling river or after the Celtic river goddess Danu – also has its source on the wild moors between Leek and Buxton. This is Dane Head, a mere trickle out of the peat moor, where the Dane begins its journey westwards to the River Mersey and out into the Irish Sea.

Another shot of the Dane near to its source.

The Dane at Three Shires Head, where the counties of Staffordshire, Cheshire and Derbyshire converge.

The river tumbles down into the Dane Valley around Gradbach and Wincle.

A tributary of the River Dane is crossed by an ancient packhorse bridge at Quarnford.

Spring sunshine at Dane Bridge.

Bartomley Farm, overlooking the River Dane at Wincle.

Folley Mill, on the River Dane, Wincle, so named because access was extremely restricted.

A view of mighty Shutlingslow from Folley Mill.

The picturesque spot known as "The Pingle" in the Dane valley.

Above: As the Dane flows through Rushton, part of its waters are utilised to feed nearby Rudyard Lake, a reservoir which serves the Macclesfield Canal. A feeder was cut some 250 years ago to take the Dane's waters to Rudyard.

Left: Close to the Dane Feeder stands this building, formerly the Hanging Gate public house but now a private residence.

Wall Hill House, Rushton, close to the Dane and the Dane Feeder.

Rudyard Lake and the village of Rudyard have been popular with tourists since the railway brought people from all over the Midlands and north west to the beauty spot. Fed by the River Dane, the Rudyard Reservoir is ideal for fishing, boating and other activities. This delightful photograph is far too early to be taken by Gerald Hine, as it shows Edwardian ladies and gents dancing at Rudyard to the accompaniment of a band.

Nearby Clough Brook, which flows through Wildboarclough before joining the Dane, photographed on a winter's day – 27 February, 1955.

Another view of Clough Brook, 27 February, 1955.

The River Lathkill's source. A scrapbook compiled by Gerald Hine in 1939 contained the following:

Lathkill! What memories that name conjures up of happy summer days spent in the cool shade of spreading beeches, vistas of glistening weirs, of silvery trout, the old mill and the memorable view of Cales Dale from above. The River Lathkill has forsaken its original course and now fluctuates between the large low cavern below Ricklow Quarries and the mouth of Cales Dale. In the spring a good head of water pours from the cavern from an underground lake forming the overflow of this subterranean source, and passing down the high narrow gorge among tumbled heaps of rock, joins the three springs at Cales Dale.

Ricklow Dale, at the head of Lathkill Dale. The waters, icy cold from the depths, maintain their crystal clearness.

Ricklow Dale, still a very popular tourist magnet.

Lathkill Dale. A series of low weirs, designed to encourage the breeding of trout, break the river's fall.

Lathkill Dale. Looking upstream the weirs have the appearance of a series of large steps.

Lathkill Dale, which was the site of a number of lead mines in the nineteenth century.

Another view of Lathkill Dale.

This view of Parson's Tor in Lathkill Dale shows the limestone strata and screes to good effect. The tor gets its name from an unfortunate vicar of Monyash, Robert Lomas who, one night in 1776, unwittingly rode over its edge and tumbled to his death on the rocks beneath.

One of Gerald's favourite walks was along the river at Conksbury Bridge in Lathkill Dale, one of the prettiest parts of the dale. In 1939 he wrote in his scrapbook:

The hand of man is evident at Conksbury, a spot where motorists pause to admire and leave their "card" behind. The fine bridge with its high narrow roadway and twin arches is a fitting background for the long curving sweep of the river.

Conksbury Bridge. The lovely river continues to Alport, where it joins the River Bradford, continuing until it flows into the River Wye near Rowsley.

The Wye flows swiftly at Monsal Dale.

Miller's Dale, another popular spot, is on the River Wye under Raven's Tor, in the parish of Tideswell, 4 miles north–west of Bakewell.

Lush vegetation surrounds the River Wye at Miller's Dale.

As the Wye continues, it loses itself among the trees as the photographer looks down at Chee Dale.

The Wye at Chee Dale.

Another important river rising around the Buxton area is the Goyt. Today the reservoir-filled Goyt Valley is a tourist's delight. This enigmatic and historic picture was taken at the Stepping Stones in the valley many years before it was flooded to build the Errwood Reservoir.

Above: Another victim of the flooding of the Goyt Valley to create the Errwood Reservoir was the Victorian, Italianate mansion of Errwood Hall, former home of the Grimshawe family. The Grimshawes were staunch Roman Catholics, and this circular shrine to St Joseph still stands in splendid isolation on the moors above the preserved ruins of the house.

Left: The interior of the chapel, showing the ceramic-tiled shrine to St Joseph, which always seems to have fresh flowers adorning it.

SIX

HERE AND THERE

G erald Hine was an avid rambler and visitor to this remarkable area. Judging from the photographs in his "Boxes of Delights", he took a camera with him whenever he could. On the next pages we take a final look at some of the many varied shots he took over the years.

Try as we might, we have been unable to identify the location of this particular photograph, or of the people on and around the horses and coach. No doubt a reader will be able to solve the problem, but the photograph, even with the damage, was just too interesting to omit.

The Cat and Fiddle Inn – the second highest public house in England, situated on the Macclesfield to Buxton road – has been photographed many times over the years. Here we see it in winter.

The Cat and Fiddle, standing at 1609 feet above the sea, must have been a welcome sight for early travellers on the Buxton-Macclesfield turnpike, as you can imagine in this other wintry photograph.

Above: Eyam will forever be known as "the Plague village" because of the "visitation" of bubonic plague between 1665–6. At the centre of the outbreak, which killed 259 of the villagers, was the twelfth-century parish church of St Lawrence, seen in this photograph.

Right: An interesting and rare feature of St Lawrence's Eyam is this eighteenth-century sundial on the outside south wall of the chancel.

The village stocks still stand on the green at Eyam, opposite Eyam Hall, home of the Wright family ever since it was built in 1676.

These cottages by the church are where the plague started, allegedly brought to Eyam in a bundle of cloth from London by a travelling tailor called George Viccars. Within days, the disease had started to spread throughout the village.

The villagers' brave answer, led by their rector William Mompesson and his non-conformist predecessor Thomas Stanley, was that to stop the disease spreading to neighbouring villages, they would impose a quarantine on movements to and from Eyam. Provisions for the villagers were left at places like Mompesson's Well, on the outskirts of the village.

The gritstone outcrop of Robin Hood's Stride, near Birchover, has the alternative local name of Mock Beggar's Hall because of its resemblance to a ruined building, especially in evening light. Evidence of early man has been found near the distinctive formation, and nearby is the Bronze Age stone circle of Nine Stones (although there are now only four).

Cratcliffe Tor lies across the ancient trackway known as the Portway, opposite Robin Hood's Stride. This massive gritstone outcrop shelters a Hermit's Cave behind a spreading yew tree at its foot. There is a medieval carving of a crucifix on the back wall of the (now railed) Hermit's Cave.

Early spring of 1956, and these ladies take a break from their rambles to feed the ducks at a farm near Tissington.

The parish church of St Mary at Tissington has a squat Norman west tower, and a Norman font and chancel arch inside. The north aisle was added in 1854, when the chancel was also rebuilt.

Fenny Bentley Hall, near Ashbourne, (now known as Cherry Orchard Farm) has a Northumbrian feel about it. The crenellated tower on the front of the house looks exactly like a pele tower from the Borders. The house was built in the fifteenth century by the Beresford family, a famous name hereabouts.

The unusually-dedicated fourteenth- and fifteenth-century parish church of St Mary and St Barlok at Norbury south of Ashbourne, is famous for its tombs of the Fitzherbert family in the beautifully-traceried chancel. These fine alabaster tombs date mainly from the fifteenth century and show the Fitzherberts in full armour.

Sutton Hall, near Macclesfield, once the home of the Lucan family, is now a popular hotel and restaurant.

Above: Little Moreton Hall near Congleton in Cheshire is perhaps the best-known example of black-and-white timber-framed architecture in the country. The drunkenly-reeling south front is seen here from the south west across the moat. The earliest part of the hall dates from the fifteenth century, but most of the decoratively-framed south front was built by John Moreton between 1560–70.

Below: This view shows the full, 68-foot length of the spectacular Long Gallery on the third storey of the Hall, which has arch-braced roof trusses and a number of original wall-painted murals depicting subjects like "Destiny" and "Fortune".

Above: Wooton Lodge in the Weaver Hills, the last outpost of the Pennines.

Below: The entrance to Wooton Lodge.

The Weaver Hills at Wooton.

Daffodils at Lyme Park, former home of the Legh family at Disley, near Stockport.

The avenue at Lyme Park.

A winter view to Hanging Gate at Higher Sutton.

Some views in the Upper Dove valley. The view to High Wheeldon.

The view towards Earl Sterndale.

The view towards Alstonefield.

Above: The parish church of St Peter at Alstonefield has a sturdy fourteenth-century Perpendicular west tower and what Pevsner describes as "enjoyable Jacobean woodwork" inside, including a two-deck pulpit dating from 1637.

Left: Charles Cotton was the co-author with Izaak Walton of the fisherman's classic, *The Compleat Angler*, first published in 1653 and never out of print since. He was a fairly-disreputable local landowner, always in debt, and this photograph shows his box pew inside Alstonefield Church.

Above: Alstonefield Hall, now a private residence, was built by John Harpur the year before the Armada in 1587. It is a substantial gabled stone Tudor house, with mullioned windows and an internal stone spiral staircase.

Right: One of the most striking features of Alstonefield Hall are the chimneys at the rear of the house (left). These triple stone-built chimneys show typical Tudor angular styling.

Hall Dale, in the valley of the Dove.

Clouds over Hall Dale.